Alfred's Basic Piano
Merry Christmas!

Willard A. Palmer ◆ Morton Manus ◆ Amanda Vick Lethco

Level 1A

This book may be used with the primer or 1st book of any method.

CONTENTS

Piano students who have had only a few months of study will enjoy playing some familiar carols as the Christmas season approaches.

MIDDLE C POSITION: *Every* carol in this book may be played with the same hand position. With the exception of the last two lines on page 15, all carols are in MIDDLE C POSITION.

PROGRESSIVE ORDER: The carols are placed in order of difficulty, with the easiest ones first. The first four carols use familiar rhythms involving only whole, dotted half, half, and quarter notes. The pieces after page 9 use the dotted quarter and eighth note rhythm that is characteristic of most Christmas carols. Students unfamiliar with the musical notation of these rhythms will usually play them correctly by memory or, if not, they can be quickly taught by rote.

RESTS: For a clean, uncluttered appearance, rests are used only when absolutely necessary.

DUETS: Every carol in this book has a duet part. These carols make excellent student-teacher or student-parent duets. Both solo and duet parts contain measure numbers for easy reference.

Merry Christmas!

STUDENTS IN LEVEL 1A of *ALFRED'S BASIC PIANO LIBRARY:* Students past page 22 of the Lesson Book are already familiar with the keys of the Middle C position. Page 2 of *MERRY CHRISTMAS!* introduces this position on the grand staff. To the carols in this book they may add two more from Level 1A — *Jolly Old Saint Nicholas* (page 14) and *Jingle Bells* (page 51).

 A General MIDI disk is available (5722), which includes a full piano recording and background accompaniment.

Illustrations by David Silverman (Painted by Cheryl Hennigar)

Middle C Position

MIDDLE C POSITION is used for all pieces in this book!

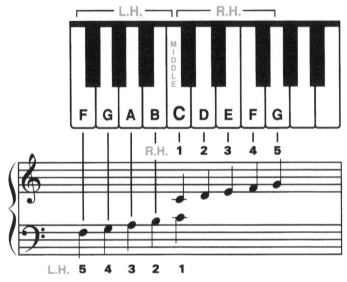

Both thumbs on MIDDLE C!

Christmas Day

Brightly

mf

1. Time for mis - tle - toe and hol - ly! Christ - mas day will soon be here!
2. Time for car - ols bright and jol - ly! Time for songs of Christ - mas cheer!

All DUET PARTS in this book are OPTIONAL. Each piece is complete as a SOLO.

DUET PART: (Student plays 1 octave higher.)

Good King Wenceslas

MIDDLE C POSITION

Moderately fast

Traditional

DUET PART: (Student plays 1 octave higher.)

We Three Kings of Orient Are

MIDDLE C POSITION

Moderately

John Henry Hopkins

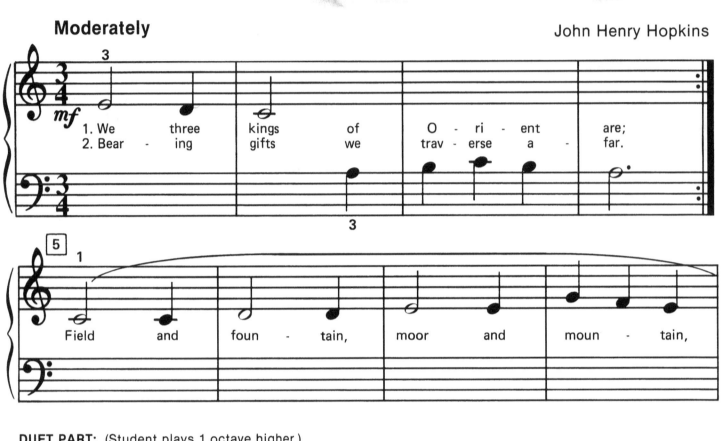

mf

1. We three kings of O - ri - ent are;
2. Bear - ing gifts we trav - erse a - far.

Field and foun - tain, moor and moun - tain,

DUET PART: (Student plays 1 octave higher.)

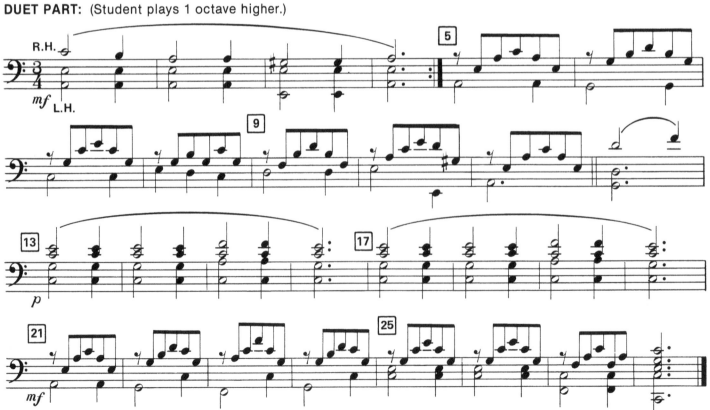

R.H.

mf L.H.

p

mf

Small notes optional

The Snow Lay on the Ground

MIDDLE C POSITION

Traditional

Moderately fast

p-f

1. The snow lay on the ground, The star
2. Ve - ni - te a - do - re - mus Do -

shone bright,_____ When Christ our Lord was
mi - num;_____ Ve - ni - te a - do -

born on Christ - mas night.
re - mus Do - mi - num.

DUET PART: (Student plays 1 octave higher.)

R.H.

p-f L.H.

Away in a Manger

MIDDLE C POSITION

Traditional

Moderately slow

A - way in a man - ger, no crib for a bed, The lit - tle Lord

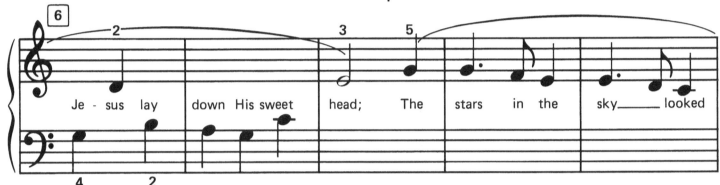

Je - sus lay down His sweet head; The stars in the sky____ looked

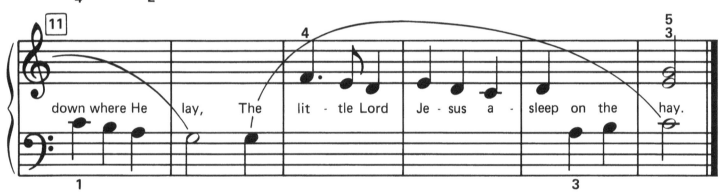

down where He lay, The lit - tle Lord Je - sus a - sleep on the hay.

DUET PART: (Student plays 1 octave higher.)

IMPORTANT!

From this page on, most of the pieces use the DOTTED QUARTER and EIGHTH NOTE rhythm.
This should be very easy because the rhythms of the songs are familiar.

The DOTTED QUARTER and EIGHTH NOTE together have a long-short feeling.

These note values, not yet introduced in *LEVEL 1A*, may be taught by rote or by memory.

O Come, All Ye Faithful

MIDDLE C POSITION

Joyfully

J. F. Wade

O come, all ye faith - ful, Joy - ful and tri - umph - ant, O

DUET PART: (Student plays 1 octave higher.)

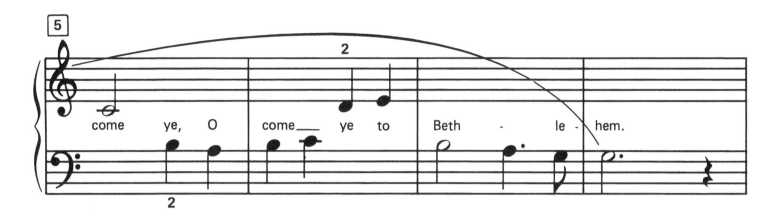

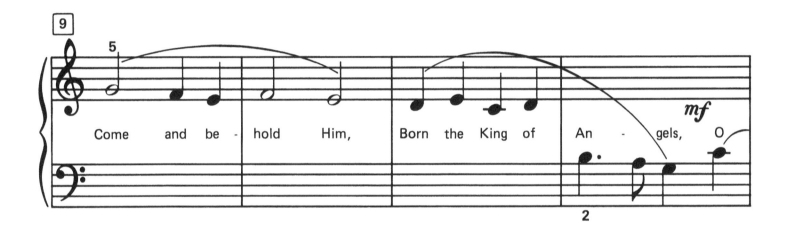

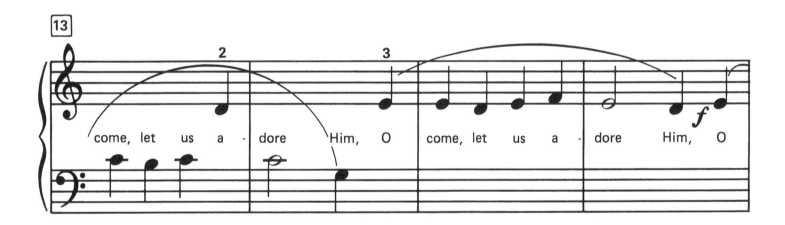

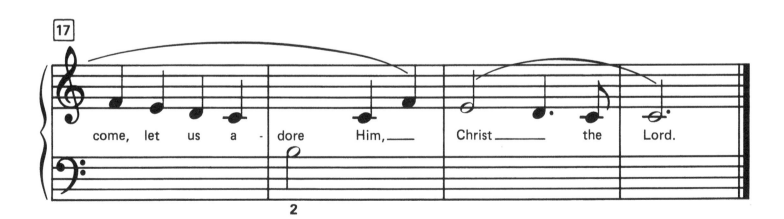

MIDDLE C POSITION (WITH F♯)

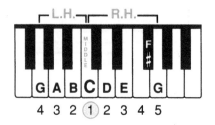

Joy to the World

Joyfully

George F. Handel

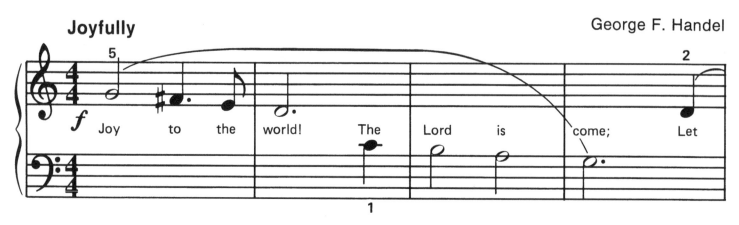

DUET PART: (Student plays 1 octave higher.)

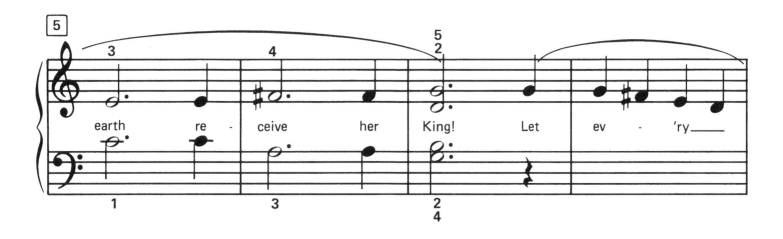

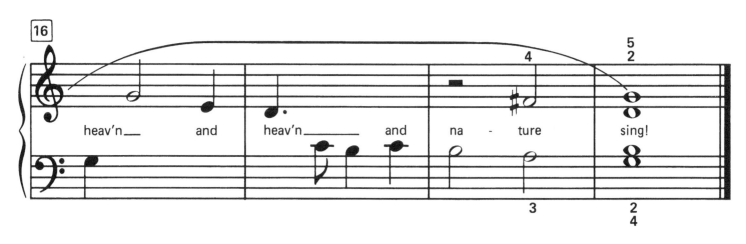

MIDDLE C POSITION (WITH B♭)

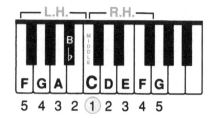

Silent Night

Franz Gruber

Gently, moderately slow

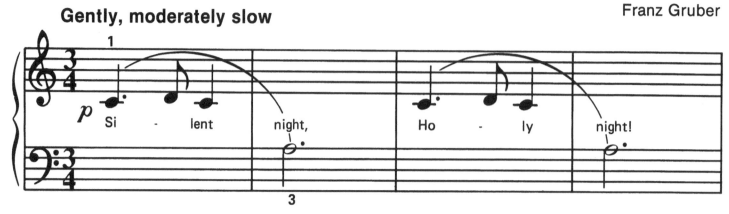

p Si - lent night, Ho - ly night!

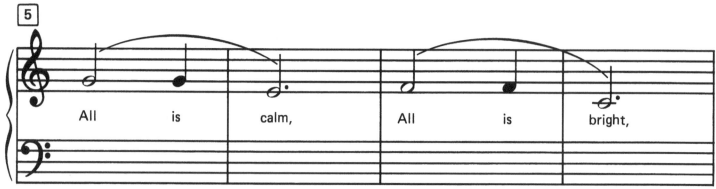

All is calm, All is bright,

DUET PART: (Student plays 1 octave higher.)

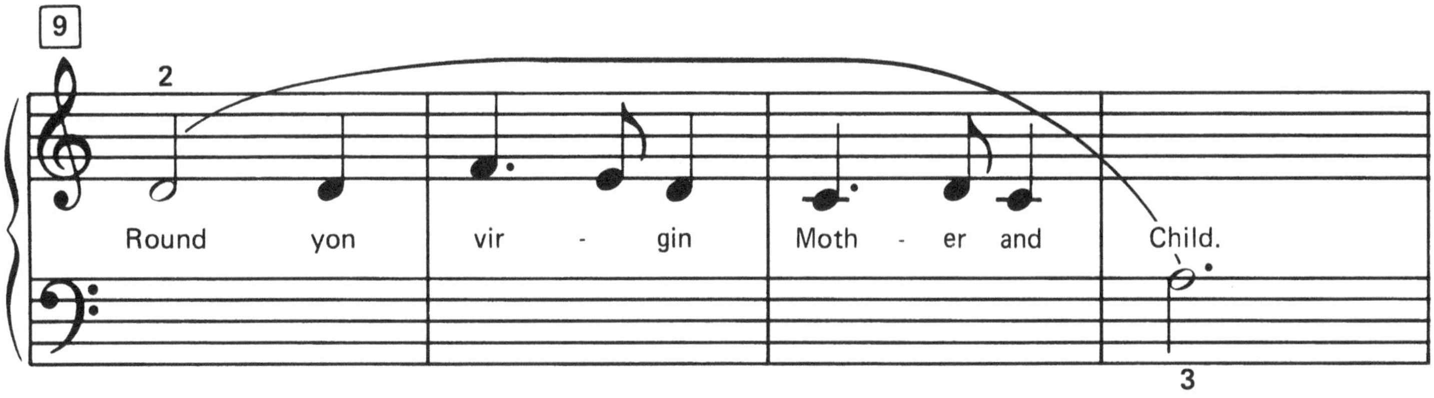
9
Round yon vir - gin Moth - er and Child.

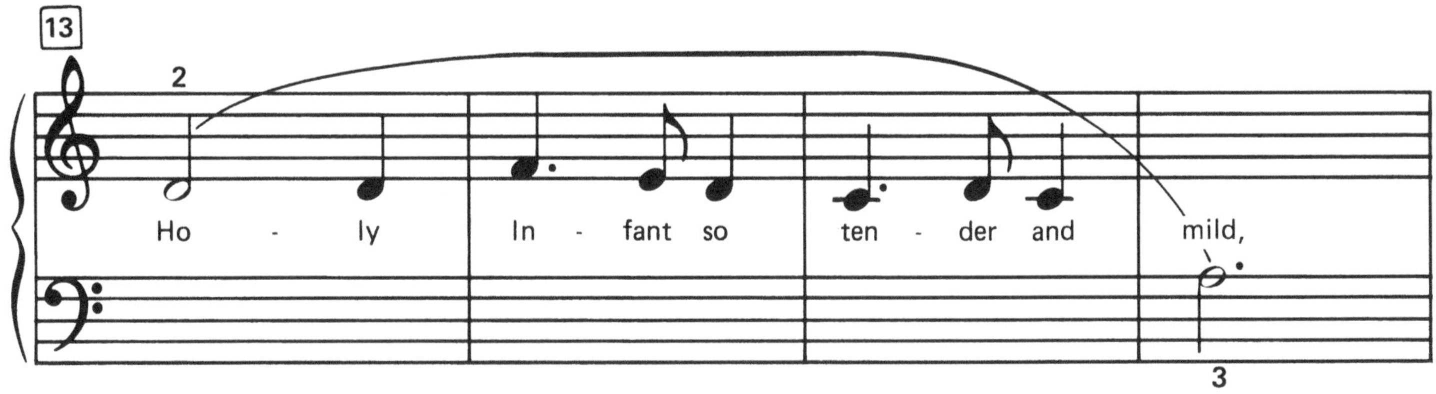
13
Ho - ly In - fant so ten - der and mild,

For the rest of the piece,
move R.H. up to the following
5 finger postion.
L.H. position does not change!

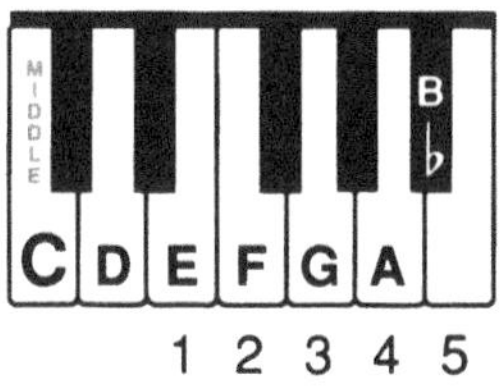
MIDDLE
B♭
C D E F G A
1 2 3 4 5

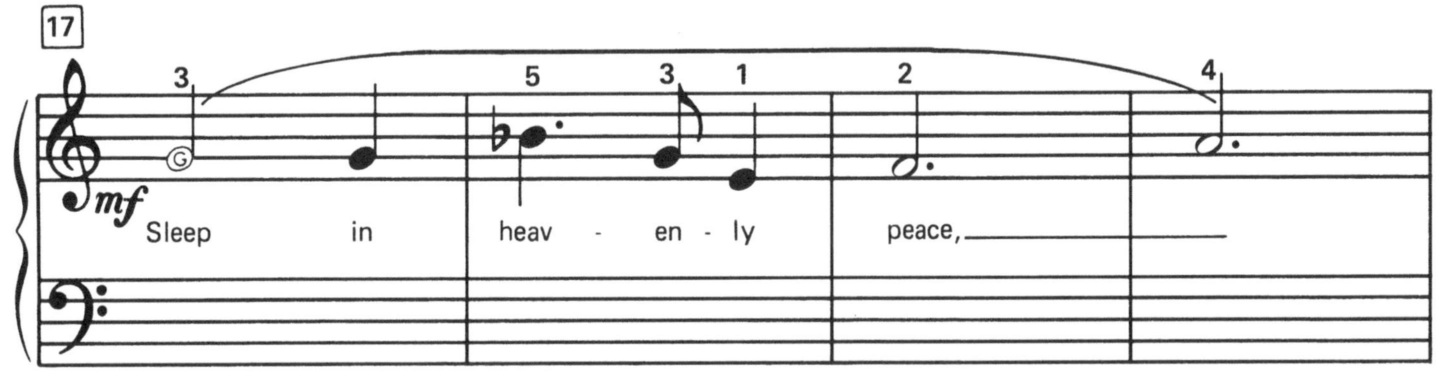
17
mf
Sleep in heav - en - ly peace,

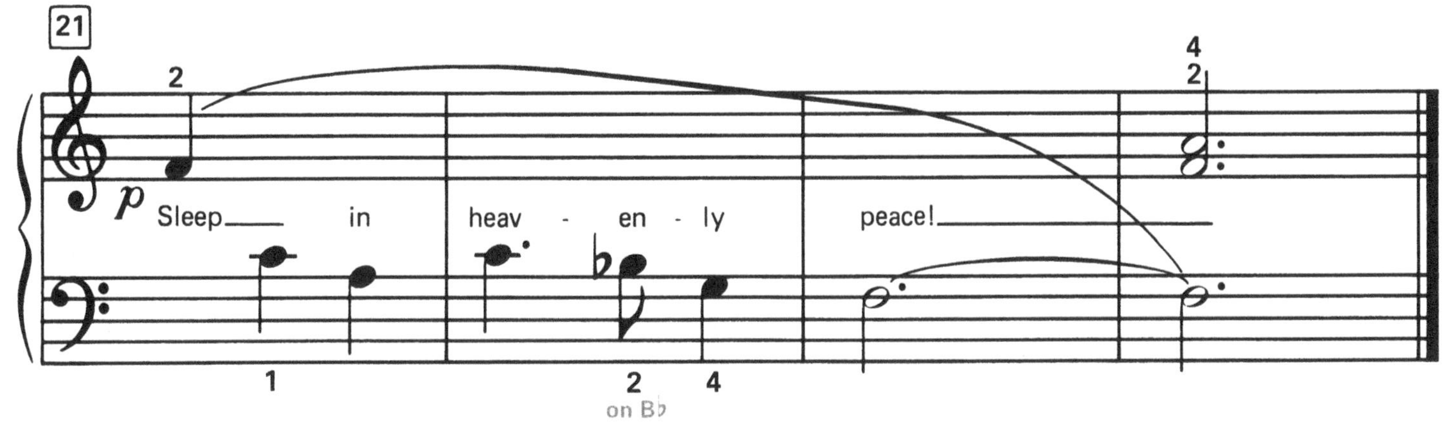
21
p
Sleep in heav - en - ly peace!
on B♭

MIDDLE C POSITION (WITH E♭)

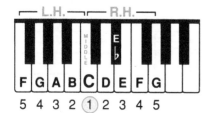

R.H. 3 plays E♮ or E♭.

The Coventry Carol

Traditional

Gently

DUET PART: (Student plays 1 octave higher.)

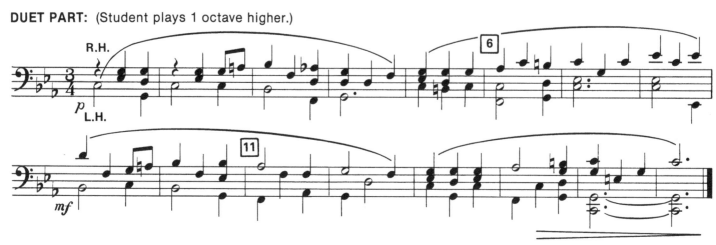